Priceless OneNote® Tips
at Your Fingertips

By

Sudhir Diddee

Copyright and Disclaimer

Send comments to diddee@outlook.com

ISBN-13: 978-1-7906-7530-2

ISBN-10: 1-7906-7530-8

To the wonderful OneNote team for creating an amazing product

Thank you

Acknowledgements

I have been fortunate to work in a great company, and continue to learn from amazing colleagues every day. What I have learned in Microsoft is the rigorous product development process and the years of user research on work and productivity that went into each feature design. The final products are awesome; however, given the plethora of features, users don't usually get around to using all of them. If you added the incremental productivity gained from all the features, you would be significantly better off. The same is true of its note taking product, OneNote®; you can save significant time each day by investing a small amount of time now in learning the features contained in OneNote®.

I would like to thank my editor Leigh-Anne, and my designer Kris Hamper. I also credit the wonderful executives, smart managers and terrific colleagues, too many to list here, with whom I am fortunate to work with and learn from every day, and who make my company truly the best place to work.

Finally, I would like to thank my wife and my kids for being extremely patient as I worked to write this book in bits and pieces. As any author knows, writing a book is hard work, and finishing the book is even harder, given all of the other priorities in life. Like everything in life, it is the result of trade-offs we make to prioritize the things we want to achieve. This book is largely about priorities, and saving time on note taking so that you can return to the more interesting things that life holds for you. I hope this book will add value (and time!) to your life.

Table of Contents

Microsoft OneNote®

One of the visions of computing was to have a paperless office. While we have made significant progress, the printers in homes and offices are still going strong, printing reams of documents every day. One of the challenges in moving to electronic documents was to capture free-form notes as one would do on a normal notepad.

Well... enter OneNote®! Microsoft OneNote® (formerly called Microsoft Office® OneNote®) is a free digital notebook on your computer. It was created about 16-17 years back to support the Tablet PC. It is a single place where you can gather your drawings, typed and handwritten notes, links, embedded documents, screen shots, and audio or video files, all on the same page, and all completely searchable and sharable. With these notebooks you can manage information overload and work together with others more effectively. Once you start using Microsoft OneNote® and get comfortable with the features, it is unlikely you will go back to using a regular notebook for note taking or information gathering.

Over the years OneNote® has gotten significantly better and is available as a free download on all mobile platforms. Hence you can use it to synch notes on your mobile phone, tablet and PC at the same time.

OneNote® is part of the Microsoft Office® 365 suite, so you may already have it! If you don't, just go to www.OneNote.com and download it onto your PC. Or you can go to any app store and download it onto your mobile device. Once you associate a Microsoft Account with the OneNote® on your PC and phone, all your notes are in synch.

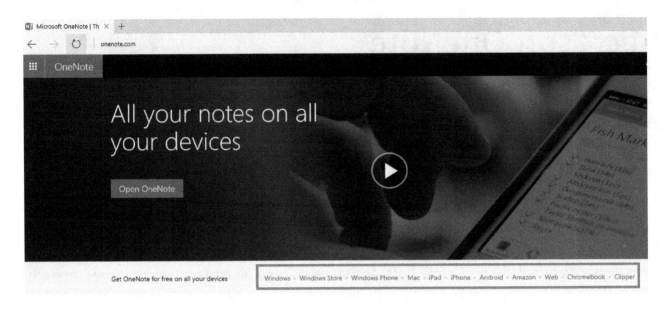

Figure 1

It takes a paradigm shift in order to shift to electronic notes. But once you make the switch, it is really convenient to be able to search your notes or easily track your tasks or to-do items. My goal in this book is to encourage you to move to electronic note taking and give it a fair shot. If you are an active OneNote® user, I can assure you – you will become a power user of OneNote® if you learn all the tricks.

If there is a tip in OneNote® that is not captured, but you think it will benefit a lot of users, feel free to send me an email and I promise to include it in the next edition of the book. I hope you enjoy the book.

Getting Started

Microsoft OneNote® Overview

OneNote® has an interesting history. When it was conceptualized, it was to capture information that was not yet solid enough to be an actual document. When you break it down, your work and personal lives are very similar, with to-do, ideas, things to remember or to explore, contacts, etc. And to put together a variety of disconnected information that can't easily be categorized, we needed a new form of information management. It would be the closest proxy to an electronic tabbed notebook. For OneNote® fans, I suggest you read Chris Pratley's blog on the genesis of OneNote® (see References in appendix).

Before we go into the features, let us quickly get an orientation of OneNote®. Think of it as a digital version of a notebook. One of the first things you will notice is that whatever you write is written forever, until you decide to delete it; i.e.: there is no **SAVE** button.

Second, it captures handwriting and drawings just as in a normal notebook. In fact, if you are using a tablet with stylus (such as Microsoft Surface), you cannot NOT use OneNote® and do justice to your tablet!

You can keep your notes here, link to or clip webpages, embed your budget spreadsheet, and note upcoming appointments. You can share all of this fluidly from your pc to your phone, and with anyone that you want.

Once you discover the power of OneNote® it is unlikely you will go back.

Note that there are 3 versions of OneNote®, all free. The app comes with the Office® 2016 suite for desktop. Then there is the OneNote® Online version at www.OneNote®.com, and finally the Universal Windows® app for desktops that can be downloaded from the web.

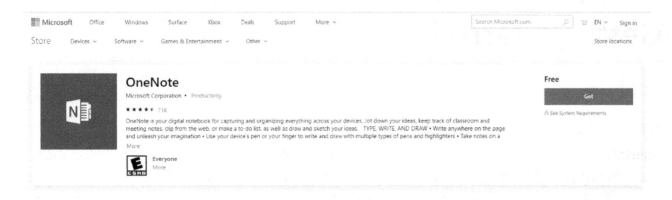

Figure 2

Per the Wikipedia entry on Office® 2019, OneNote® will be retired from the suite starting in Office® 2019. OneNote® 2016 can be installed as an optional feature on the Office® Installer; however, the only OneNote® app for PC desktops going forward will be the Universal Windows® app that is currently available for Windows® 10.

1. OneNote® structure

The best way to think of OneNote® is as the digital equivalent of a tabbed notebook, with several pages within each section. Here are a few examples of usage, to kick start your imagination.

You might create a OneNote® notebook for that upcoming 5-country trip to Europe. Your notebook might have 7 sections, with a few pages in each section:

➢ General info (e.g.: a broad overview of the trip as a whole)
➢ Emergency info (e.g.: passport and credit card info, emergency contacts)
➢ Croatia
➢ Greece
➢ Spain
➢ Portugal
➢ Italy

In each country's section, you might have the following pages:

- Air/car/rail/hotel reservations
- Maps and tourist attractions
- Embassy/consulate information

- Customary Dos and Don'ts
- Public holidays

Another use: organize it for notes, using OneNote® sections for class subjects, and the pages for lessons:

Chemistry
- Lesson 1
- Lesson 2
- Assignment 1

Physics
- Lesson 1
- Lesson 2

Alternately, you could have a OneNote® notebook for meeting notes:

Departmental meetings
- January
- February

Plan party
- Food
- Entertainment

Or research your family tree! This app has endless uses! You don't have to be nearly this organized, either. This app was made to dump information into, so you can categorize it some other time. (Or not.)

2. New note or basic note

You can use Microsoft OneNote® alongside another program simultaneously. While in any other program or website, press these keys (the Windows logo key is at bottom left on a PC keyboard):

Windows Logo Key + N*

This will start a new Microsoft OneNote® note, which can co-exist on the page. It is ideal if you are on a website or a conference call and want to take quick notes.

All the notes will be saved in a section of your notebook called Quick Notes.

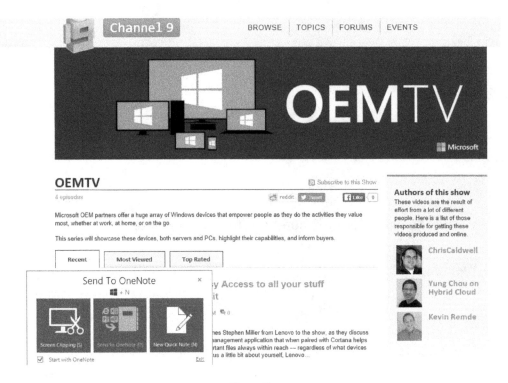

Figure 3

The OneNote® window appears over your webpage and you can take notes while browsing the page. Very handy!

Figure 4

*See appendix for handy list of Microsoft OneNote® shortcuts!

3. Pages

In OneNote® you can add pages as you go. To add a page, just click on the "+ Add Page" symbol as highlighted below, and it creates a page called Untitled Page by default.

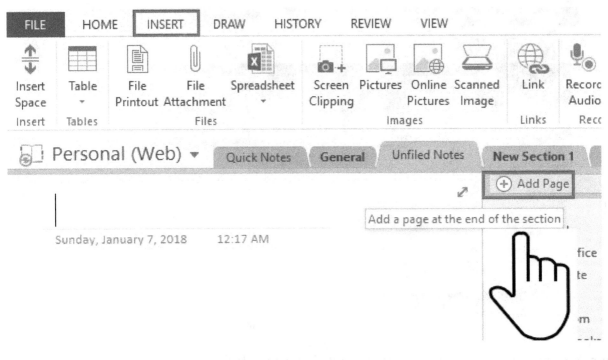

Figure 5

To rename a page, just right-click and you get options to either Rename Page, Move/Copy or make it a Subpage. (A subpage might be one presentation at a full-day conference, for example.)

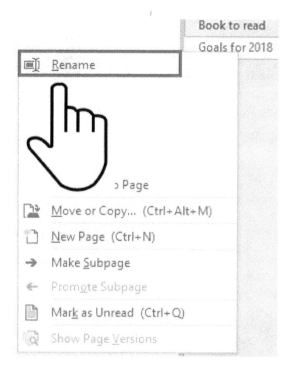

Figure 6

4. Rule lines

One of the challenges of people transitioning from physical to digital notebooks is missing the sense of the actual notebook or paper. Toward this, one option in OneNote® is to use rule lines.

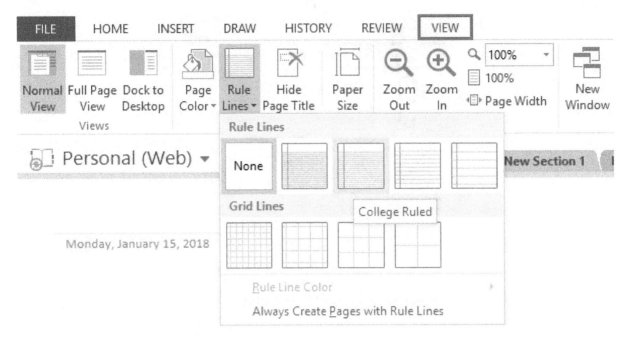

Figure 7

You can choose the type of rule lines, from a typical legal pad's lines to grid lines.

Ruled page

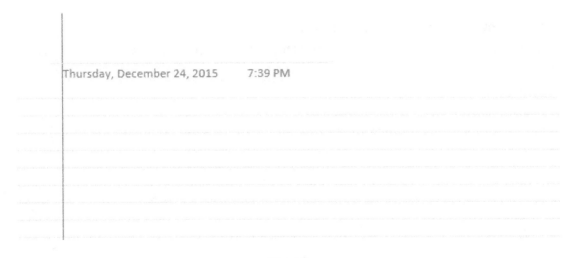

Figure 8

Grid Lines

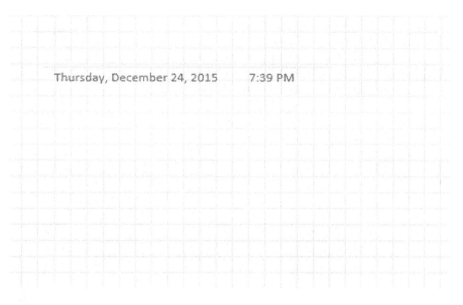

Figure 9

5. Page color

You always have the option to change the color of the page.

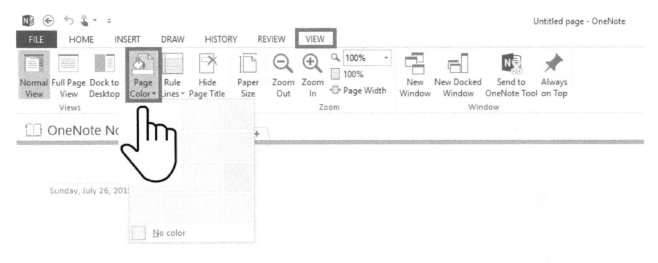

Figure 10

6. Paper size

You can define the paper size for OneNote®. Go to **View**, **Paper Size**, and select the right paper size in the drop-down window.

Figure 11

You can use this feature to adjust your notes depending on the printouts you might make.

7. Sections

Just as you have sections in a physical notebook, In OneNote® you can have sections for various subjects or topics, e.g.: Work, Home, Reading List, etc. To add a section:

Step 1 - Click on the + symbol next to the section header.

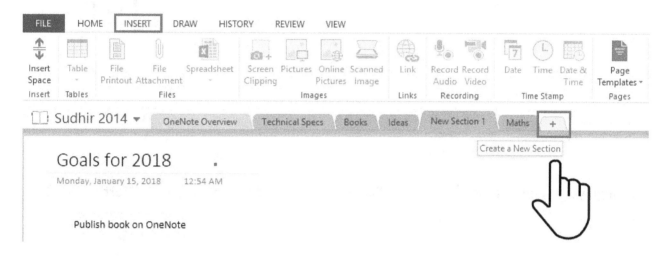

Figure 12

Step 2 - Type the name of your new section:

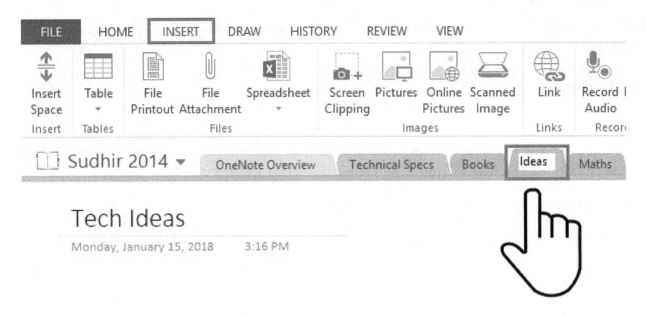

Figure 13

8. Section colors

To change your section's tab color, **right-click** the section and change to your preferred color.

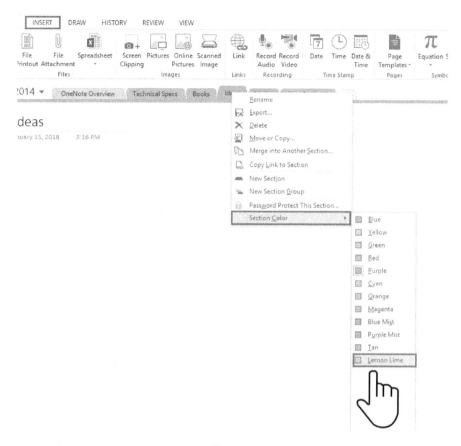

Figure 14

9. Protect a section

As you start to use Microsoft OneNote® more and realize its utility, you will soon start aggregating all kinds of information. You will find yourself saving information such as your passwords to websites, confirmations of your online orders, scanned receipts etc.

One nice feature of OneNote® is the ability to protect a section by locking it.

Step 1 – Right-click the section you want to protect

Step 2 – On the pop-up menu, scroll to **Password Protect This Section**

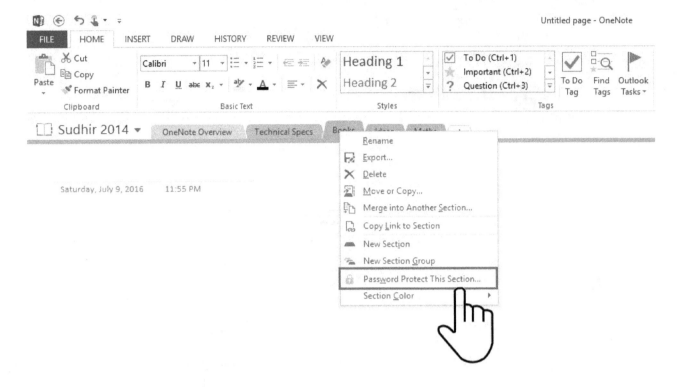

Figure 15

Step 3 – Set the password for the section. If the section is already password protected, OneNote®
will prompt you to enter the password and give you an option to remove it.

Figure 16

Power Tip: You need to unlock password-protected sections before the content is searchable.

10. Page templates

OneNote® has certain prebuilt templates which give you a head start on notes and provide consistency. Page templates are especially useful if you tend to follow a certain structure for your meetings or notes.

You can choose templates from the broad groupings of Academic, Business, and Home. To use a prebuilt template, choose Insert, then Page Templates:

Figure 17

In the Templates task pane, click the small arrows next to the category names to expand them. To apply a template, scroll down the list and select its name.

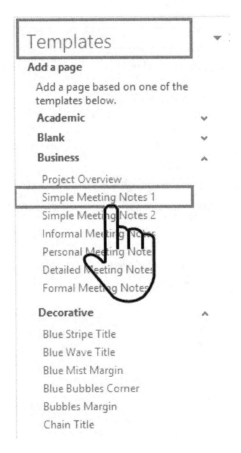

Figure 18

For example, the **Business > Simple Meeting Notes 1** template gives you a prepopulated page like the one below.

Project Overview

Sunday, July 10, 2016   1:14 AM

Project Name:
Company Name:
Presenter Name:

Description
Describe the project in non-technical terms.

Project Goals
- Ultimate goal of project
- Relationship to other projects
- High-level timing goals

Description
- Describe the project in non-technical terms.

Team/Resources
- State assumptions about resources allocated to this project
- People
- Equipment
- Locations
- Support & outside services
- Manufacturing
- Sales

Procedures

Figure 19

To use any page as your custom template, go to the Page templates and scroll to the bottom to "save current page as a template."

Figure 20

11. Stylus inputs

Not many people know the history of OneNote®. It was created for the Tablet PC, which came with a stylus pen. Over the years as OneNote® improved, the whole interface technology for Windows® changed, and with the advent of Touch OS, every Touch PC tablet can take advantage of the touch mode.

The default color of the stylus is black. However, if you want to change the color of the stylus, just click on DRAW and change to your preferred color.

Figure 21

12. Pin your favorite pens to the top

You can easily add your favorite pens to the Quick Access menu from the **Draw** tab:

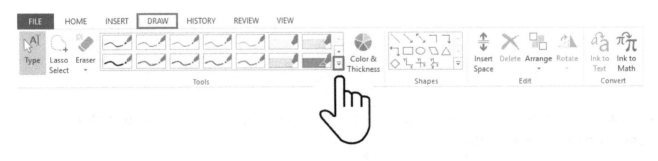

Figure 22

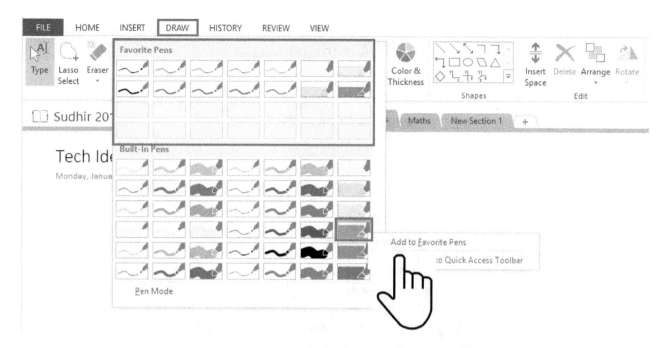

Figure 23

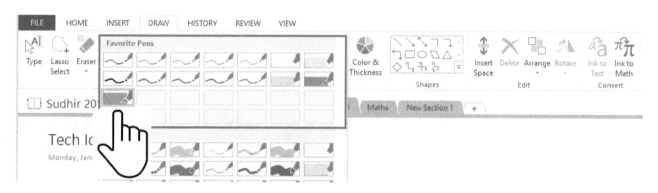

Figure 24

13. Windows® 10 Quick Note

One of the nice little enhancements in Windows® 10 has been the introduction of Quick Notes and deeper integration to OneNote®. All you need to do is type the Windows® logo key (lower left corner of PC keyboard) and N, and it will launch a mini menu that gives you the option to take a Quick Note, take a screen clipping, or send it to OneNote®.

Figure 25

Getting Productive

14. Ink to text

One cool feature of Microsoft OneNote® is the ability to convert your writing or any ink to text. Hence, if you hand-write something in OneNote®, you can just select the text, right-click and choose **Ink to Text** to convert it to typed text.

15. Copy Text from a picture

This is a hidden little feature in plain sight. You can copy text from an image in Microsoft OneNote® by right-clicking and selecting **Copy Text from Picture**.

You can also capture the text in an image to printed text by just right-clicking the image.

As a great observer of nature, Gaudí was
familiar with the way that cosmic movements
together with the power of gravity generate
a series of spiral movements on the Earth
that are also found in the animal and vegetable
kingdoms. Attracted by these phenomena,
Gaudí used the spiral in structures and deco-
rations on most of his works.

1 Snail shell | 2 Top of the staircase in Casa Milà | 3
Spiral staircase | 4 Ceiling in Casa Batlló | 6 Model. A
falling winged locust tree seed (Robinia pseudo-acacia)
describes a cylindrical helix similar to the spiral staircases in

Figure 26

You then get a menu where you can select Copy Text from Picture.

24

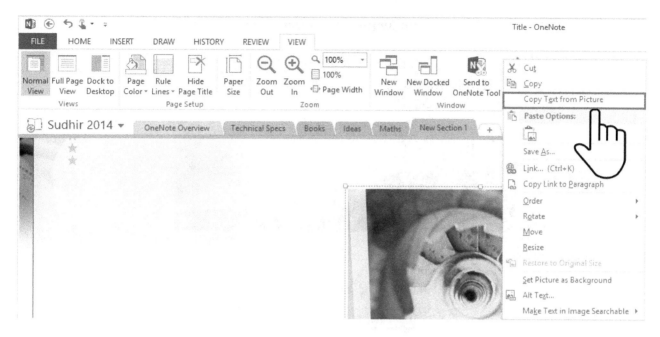

Figure 27

16. Search within an Image

Microsoft OneNote® can search within a screen image. How cool is that? Just click **CTRL + F.**
Here I am searching for the term OneNote:

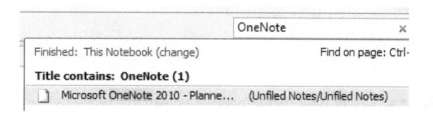

Figure 28

This is how the results will appear:

Figure 29

17. Basic math input

Microsoft OneNote® allows for basic mathematical calculations, which can be handy. Place the cursor after the equal sign (=) in each example below and press the spacebar:

3*9=

54/6=

18. Insert math equations

For students, one useful feature is to be able to insert a math equation. For example, if you want to enter the area of a circle: click on Insert, Equation, then select **Area of Circle** as below.

Figure 30

And the page looks like this.

Math Equations

Sunday, July 10, 2016   1:52 AM

$$A = \pi r^2$$

$$x = \frac{-b \pm \sqrt{b^2 - 4ac}}{2a}$$

Figure 31

19. Solve math equations--Ink to Math

This is a really cool tip and I wish I'd had it when I was in school. Let's say you have to solve a simple math equation.

Step 1 – Go to OneNote.com and log into your OneNote® notebook.

Step 2 – Type or even hand write, for example, x/2 + x/3 = 1/6.

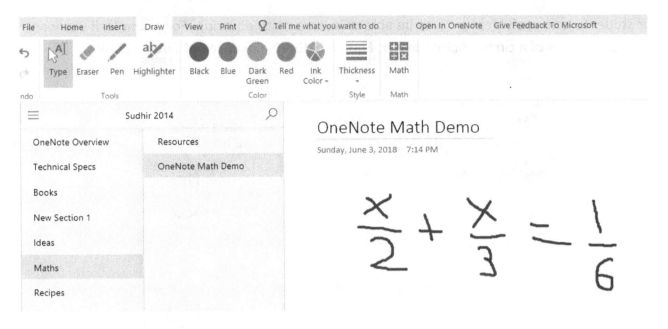

Figure 32

Step 3 – On the Draw tab, select the equation and click on the **Math** (or **Ink to Math**) button:

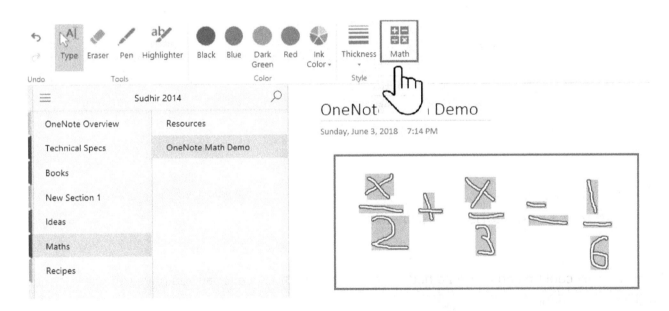

Figure 33

Step 4 – You will see an option to solve for the variable 'x' and a prompt to see the steps:

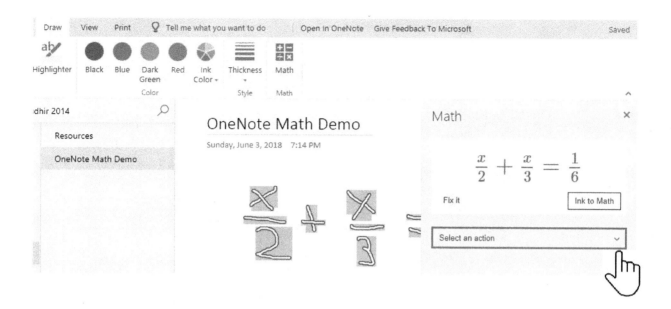

Figure 34

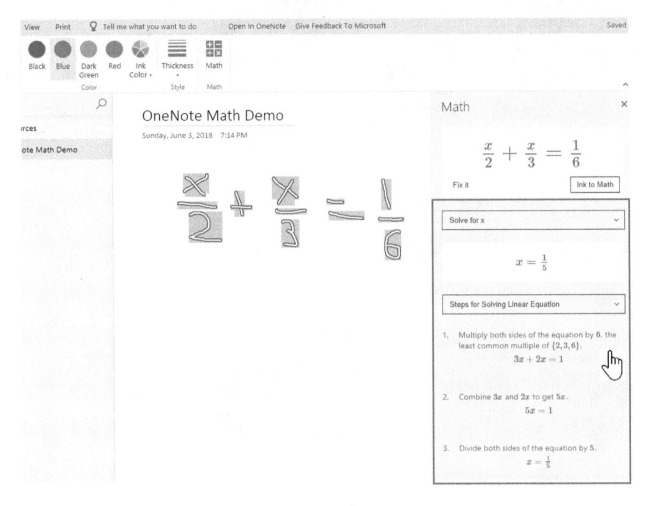

Figure 35

20. Automatically adding the source link

Whenever you paste content from a website into a OneNote® page, OneNote® automatically pastes the source link into the note. For example, when I copy content from the blog below, OneNote® automatically pastes the source into the notes.

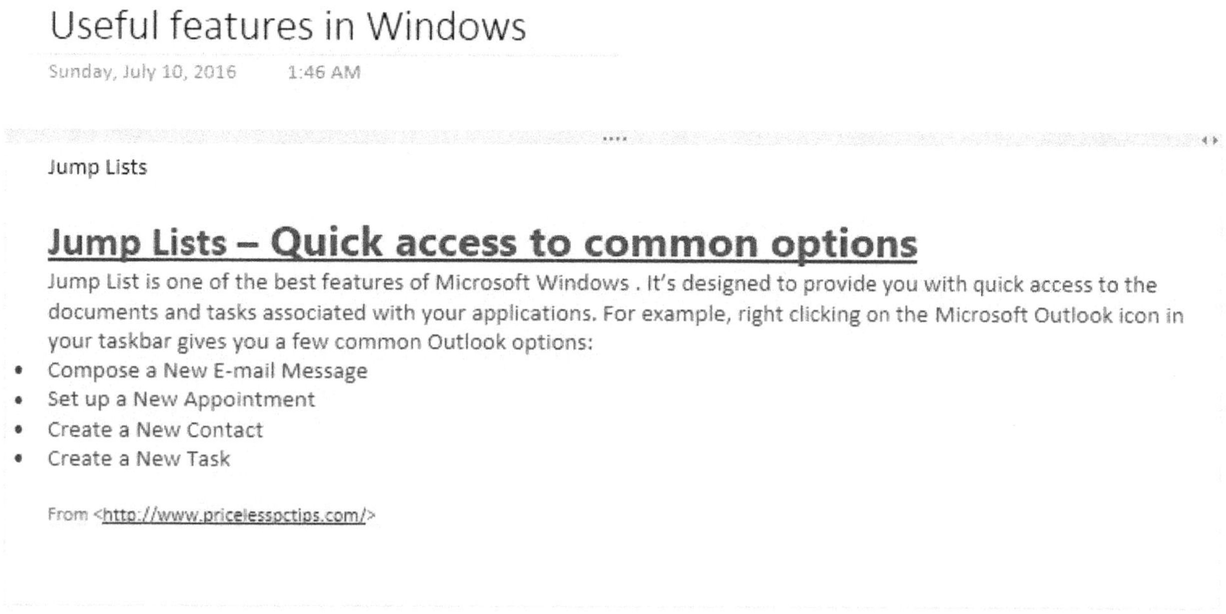

Useful features in Windows

Sunday, July 10, 2016   1:46 AM

Jump Lists

Jump Lists – Quick access to common options

Jump List is one of the best features of Microsoft Windows . It's designed to provide you with quick access to the documents and tasks associated with your applications. For example, right clicking on the Microsoft Outlook icon in your taskbar gives you a few common Outlook options:

- Compose a New E-mail Message
- Set up a New Appointment
- Create a New Contact
- Create a New Task

From <http://www.pricelesspctips.com/>

Figure 36

This is VERY useful when, say, you are performing secondary research and need to cite the source.

21. Change the location of page tabs from right to left

The default location of OneNote® tabs is on the right. The idea was to mimic the actual tabs in a physical notebook.

However, given that users are now familiar with websites and the common left-hand navigation bars, people may prefer having the navigation bar on the left. You can simply change the position of the page tabs from right to left:

Step 1 – Click on **File**, **Options**

Step 2 – Under options click on **Display** and check the box titled "**Page tabs appear on left**"

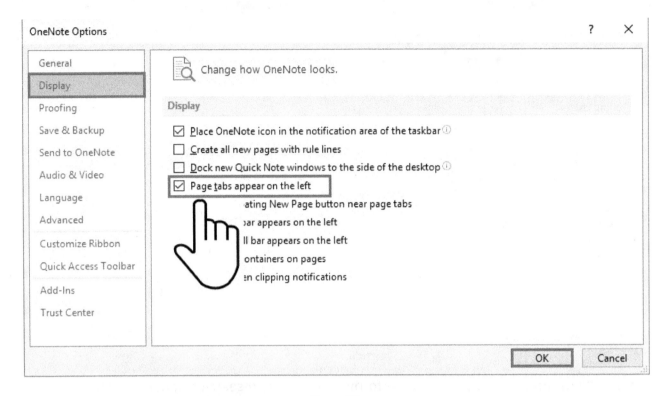

OneNote Options

General	Change how OneNote looks.
Display	
Proofing	Display
Save & Backup	☑ Place OneNote icon in the notification area of the taskbar ⓘ
Send to OneNote	☐ Create all new pages with rule lines
Audio & Video	☐ Dock new Quick Note windows to the side of the desktop ⓘ
Language	☑ Page tabs appear on the left
Advanced	...ating New Page button near page tabs
Customize Ribbon	...ar appears on the left
Quick Access Toolbar	...ll bar appears on the left
Add-Ins	...ontainers on pages
Trust Center	...en clipping notifications

OK   Cancel

Figure 37

Step 3 – Click **OK,** or else your changes are not applied.

22. Linking to another page/Creating table of contents

Say you have related topics within your notebook that need to reference each other. You can do so easily by linking to a second OneNote® page. Right-click on your original page, choose **Copy Link to a Page,** and paste the resulting link onto the second page.

You can use this function to create a table of contents. Unlike Microsoft Word® that automatically creates a table of contents, you have to create one in OneNote®. Just right-click on your original page, choose **Copy Link to a Page,** and paste the link onto your table of contents page. You can quickly build your own table of contents, as seen below:

Figure 38

The final Table of Content looks like this.

Figure 39

23. Microsoft OneNote® in full-screen mode

If you are working on a notebook page and need more screen area, hit the **F11** key. See the difference in the two notes here? It always helps to declutter the screen and focus on the meeting or task at hand.

Normal Screen mode:

Figure 40

Full screen mode:

Figure 41

The advantage of full screen mode is that it hides all your distractions so that one can focus at the task at hand or the meeting one is attending.

24. Tag and categorize items

You can place a custom tag on any item on a OneNote® page. This is so handy. For example, when you perform a brain dump of all of your pending items, you will end up with an assorted list. You can then tag each item with a category.

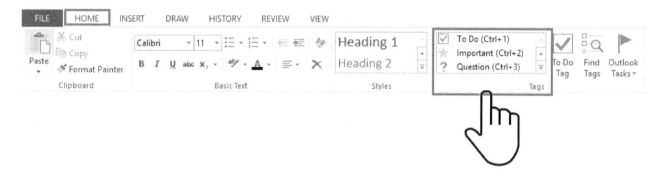

Figure 42

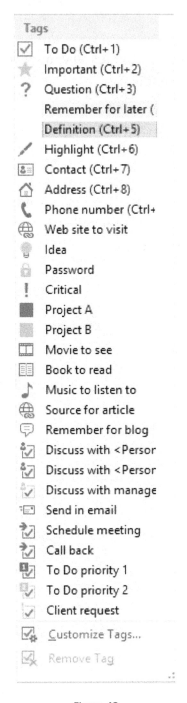

Figure 43

The full list of available categories is fairly rich, providing for a nice level of detail:

Your list might look like this:

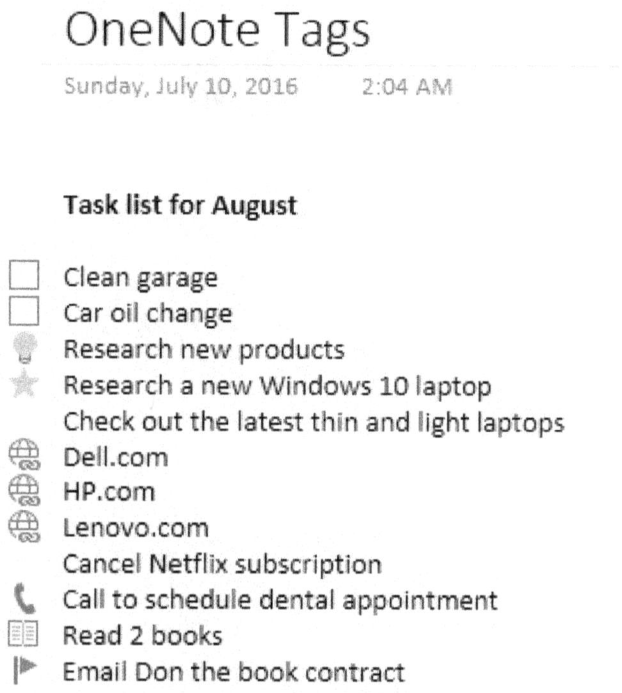

OneNote Tags

Sunday, July 10, 2016   2:04 AM

Task list for August

- ☐ Clean garage
- ☐ Car oil change
- 💡 Research new products
- ⭐ Research a new Windows 10 laptop
- Check out the latest thin and light laptops
- 🌐 Dell.com
- 🌐 HP.com
- 🌐 Lenovo.com
- Cancel Netflix subscription
- 📞 Call to schedule dental appointment
- 📖 Read 2 books
- 🚩 Email Don the book contract

Figure 44

Now most of your task items are in categories. This is handy at those times when you find yourself with a spare 20 minutes and can quickly summon all of the phone calls you have been needing to make. This is invaluable as your OneNote® content expands.

25. Search tags

Microsoft OneNote® allows you to search by the different tag types you have assigned to each item. The search capability is fairly robust, and you can search by tag type, age of note, note location (sections within a notebook, or within all notebooks), and other options.

Your search will result in a Tags Summary, which I've set here to automatically sort by tag type; hence all to-do items are together, as are all important action items, etc.

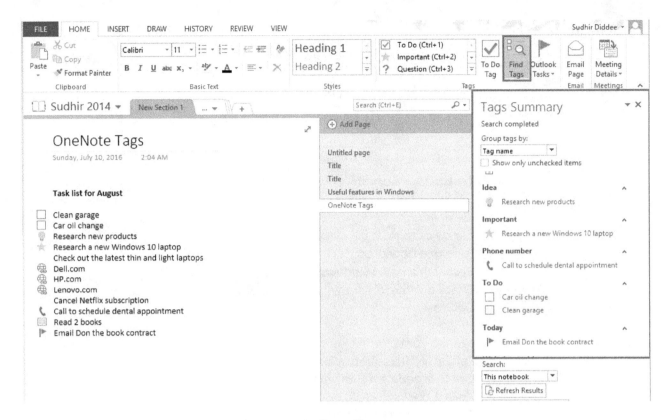

Figure 45

This is invaluable for meetings and classes, where at varying points you may find you have either follow-up or action items. When you review your notes later, you can easily create a Tags Summary page by choosing: **File, Find Tags, Create Summary Page**.

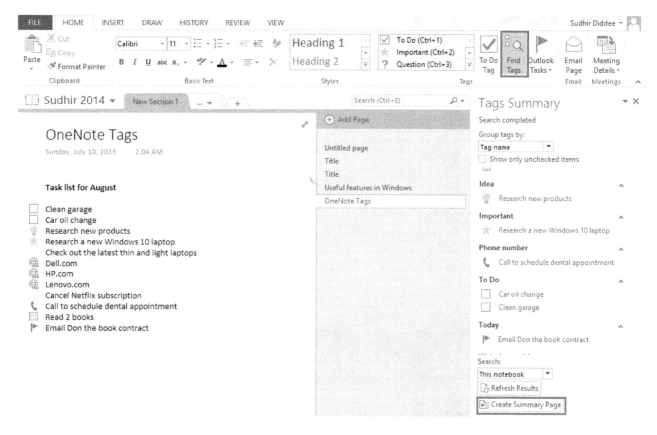

Figure 46

The Tags Summary page looks like this:

Book to read
    📖 Read 2 books

Homework

    🏠

Idea
    💡 Research new products

Important
    ⭐ Research a new Windows® 10 laptop

Phone number
    📞 Call to schedule dental appointment

To Do

- ☐ Car oil change
- ☐ Clean garage

Today

- ⚑ Email Don the book contract

Web site to visit

- 🌐 Dell.com
- 🌐 HP.com
- 🌐 Lenovo.com

26. Simple notes search

To search through content in OneNote®, just type **CTRL+E.** The context shifts to a search window and you can define the scope. OneNote® search is pretty exhaustive and returns the results across the contents of all pages, sections, and even all notebooks.

Power tip: any password-protected sections will be excluded unless they are unlocked at the time of the search.

27. Advanced notes search

OneNote® has ability to do advanced search. When you type **CTRL+E,** you will see the search results as shown below; for example, I searched for the Windows® shortcut to Lock the Device, and it is **the Windows logo key + L.**

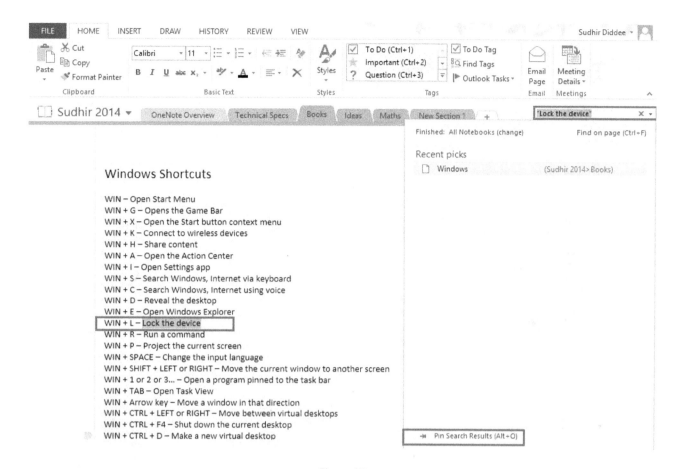

Figure 47

If you click on the **Pin Search Results** option, or type in Alt+O, you are presented with advanced Search options. (See appendix for list of Microsoft OneNote® shortcuts.)

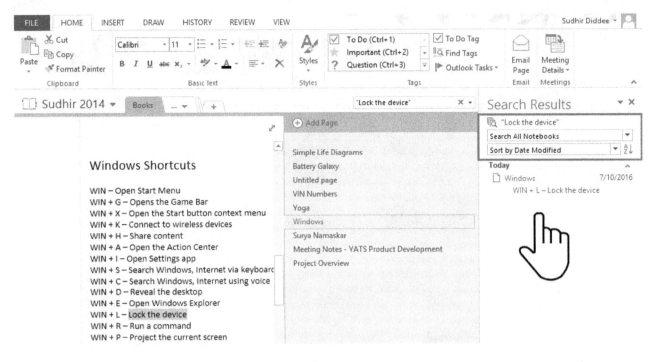

Figure 48

28. Dock to Desktop

One terrific feature of OneNote® is to have it open and docked off to your right in a separate window while you are researching your next fabulous trip on various websites, or in a conference-call application like Skype for Business. This allows you to take notes and remain focused.

Here I have a OneNote® window docked to the right of a page on edX. This way I can follow the lecture and keep typing notes.

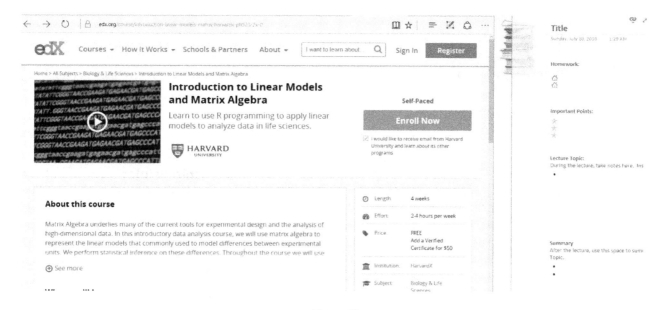

Figure 49

To dock a window, simply type **CTRL+ALT+D** and any page will dock to the right of your computer screen.

29. Emailing notes

If you become addicted to Microsoft OneNote® as I have, you will find yourself taking all your meeting notes in OneNote®, creating tasks and more. If you want to share your meeting notes by sending an email consisting of the OneNote® page, type **Ctrl + Shift + E**. Click the button in the toolbar, choose your recipients, and your notes are easily distributed without any retyping.

This is extremely handy; you can send the meeting notes to participants right after the meeting vs. having to copy and paste your notes into an email.

43

OneNote® and Microsoft Outlook®

30. Send to OneNote® from Microsoft Outlook®

OneNote® is one of my favorite Microsoft products, especially for organizing information. But for most people, another program, Microsoft Outlook®, has become the universal information repository.

One common excuse I hear from people having Outlook® open 10 hours a day is... "All my information is in Outlook!" While I cannot disagree, one of the coolest features of Microsoft Outlook® is its seamless integration with OneNote®.

On a typical day an average office worker receives about 100 emails. If you are in a senior role, the email volume could be up to 200 emails a day. However, only 2% to 4% of the emails have content you need to actually refer to; e.g.: links to internal reporting sites, new policies that you may need to refer to, or good emails you need to refer back to.

So, all you need to do is move those to OneNote®. And in any given year you will have only about 500 pages max of one notebook in OneNote®. You can maintain one notebook per year. For example, when I received my billing statement for renewal of my MSDN subscription, I just moved it to OneNote® as a proof of the payment confirmation.

Figure 50

In case you need to reuse the material – no need to cut and paste the content back into email. Just open the page in OneNote® and press **CTRL+SHIFT+E** to email the page to the recipient. This kind of seamless integration makes the Microsoft Office® suite-enabled productivity priceless.

31. Integration of tasks with Microsoft Outlook®

Perhaps the best part of OneNote® is the native integration with Microsoft Outlook®, the powerful productivity suite that integrates your email, calendar, tasks, and contacts.

To demonstrate this integration, we have opened OneNote and searched for **Outlook Tasks**, next to **Find Tags**.

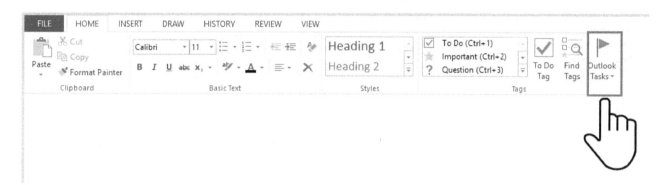

Figure 51

On our "Task list for August," created in OneNote, we have assigned one of the tasks a tag; look for the small red flag next to the task, "Email Don the book contract."

Task list for August

☐ Clean garage
☐ Car oil change
💡 Research new products
⭐ Research a new Windows® 10 laptop
   Check out the latest thin and light laptops
🌐 Dell.com
🌐 HP.com
🌐 Lenovo.com
   Cancel Netflix subscription
📞 Call to schedule dental appointment
📖 Read 2 books
🚩 Email Don the book contract

When we navigate over to the Tasks section within Microsoft Outlook®, we will see that a task entry has already been created, effortlessly.

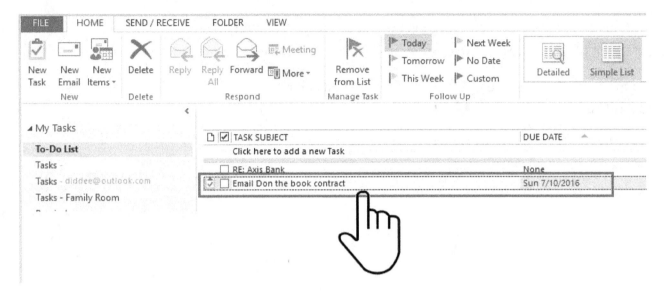

Figure 52

You can flag OneNote® items as Tasks to be tracked in Microsoft Outlook® with just this shortcut **Ctrl + Shift + 1**. The task is then created in Microsoft Outlook®, and the done/not done status is kept in sync with OneNote®, where it originated.

Again, you create a task by typing **CTRL + SHIFT + 1.**

Figure 53

It then shows up in your Task list in Microsoft Outlook® automatically. Cool, huh?

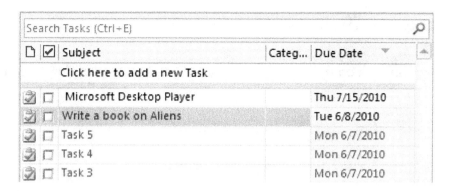

Figure 54

32. Linked Microsoft Outlook® meeting notes

In any meeting, you can click on the OneNote® icon within Microsoft Outlook to create linked meeting notes.

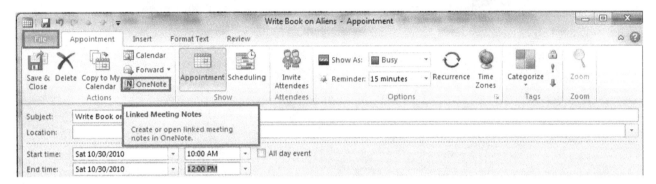

Figure 55

Clicking on the icon gives you an option to insert the notes into the right category:

Figure 56

It automatically creates a ready-to-go note with the meeting title, date, and attendees, generated from Microsoft Outlook's calendar:

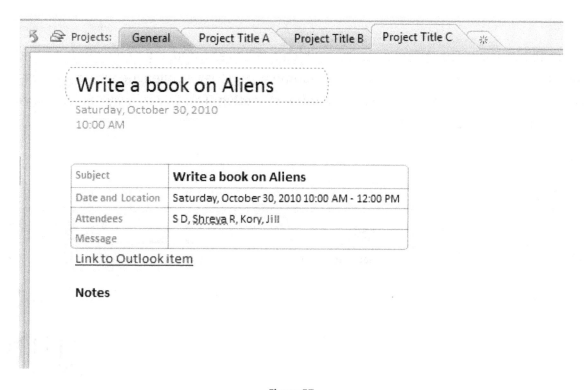

Figure 57

Advanced Features

33. Record audio

There are times when you attend a meeting which can be recorded, e.g.: new market trends on consumer electronics or a talk on career development. Say that a colleague who could not attend wanted you to take notes or, better still, record the meeting. The easiest way: use the **Record Audio** feature of OneNote®, on the Insert tab.

Step 1

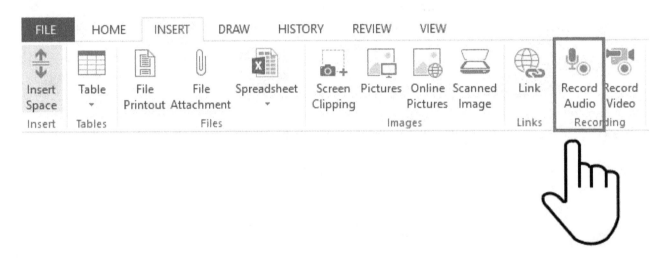

Figure 58

Step 2 – You will see the menu specific to recording, playback etc.

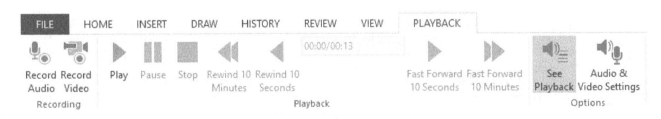

Figure 59

To share the audio recording just email the page to your colleague or if the file is too large share via an online file sharing site (e.g. www.onedrive.com) or your company intranet.

34. Record video

Similar to the audio, you can easily record and share video recordings in OneNote®.

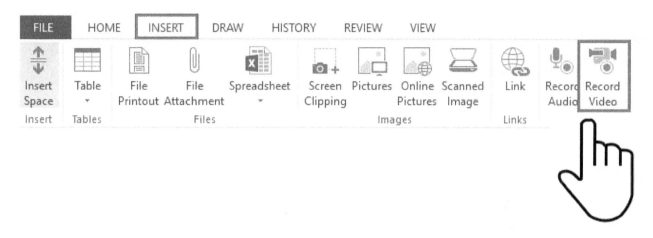

Figure 60

This is useful if you have to record a podcast, or you need to practice a speech. You will see all the same controls for as for audio.

35. Search within audio and video

Here is a killer feature of OneNote®! You can actually make your audio/video searchable. Yes, Microsoft OneNote® allows you to search for a spoken word in an audio or video. Start by going into OneNote 's options for Audio and Video:

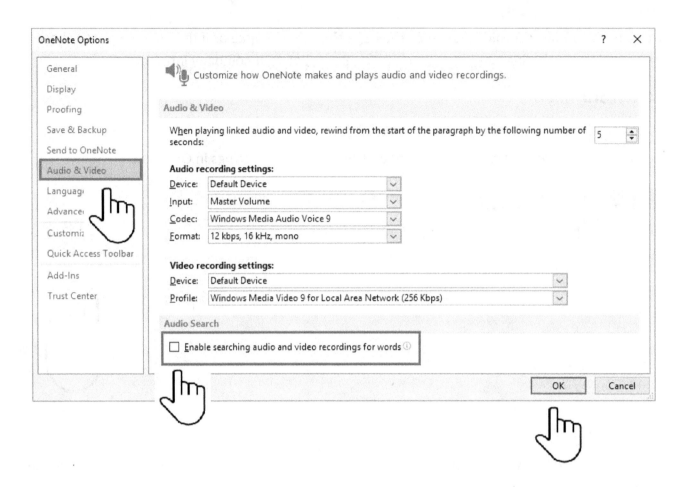

Figure 61

Step 2 – Click on **Enable Audio Search**

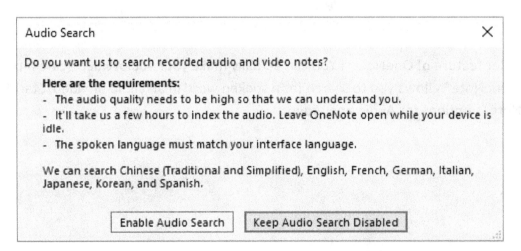

Figure 62

36. Clip a browser

Often we are researching the Web or browsing and come across a cool image, idea or itinerary that someone has researched and posted that you want to save for reference. The usual way would be to bookmark and remember what the book mark is about. Better: use OneNote® Clipper. Think of OneNote® Clipper as a camera for the web. Here is how to get it:

Step 1 – Go to www.OneNote.com/clipper

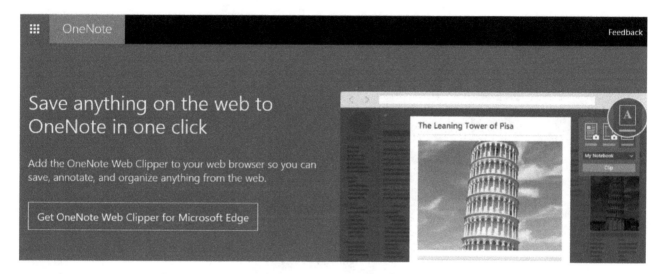

Figure 63

Step 2: Click on the link: Get OneNote® Web Clipper for Microsoft Edge. You will be prompted to download the Microsoft Edge extension from the Microsoft Store.

Figure 64

If you are using Google Chrome you will see the following link:

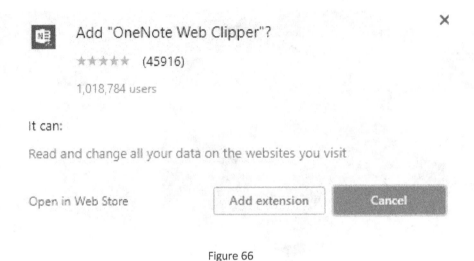

Figure 65

For Google Chrome you will see the following pop-up to add the extension to your browser

Figure 66

Step 3: Click to turn on the new extension for OneNote® Clipper:

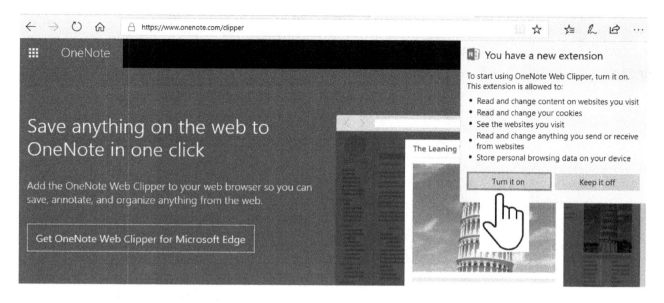

Figure 67

You will see the following prompt and a OneNote® icon on your browser:

Congratulations! OneNote Web Clipper is ready to use.

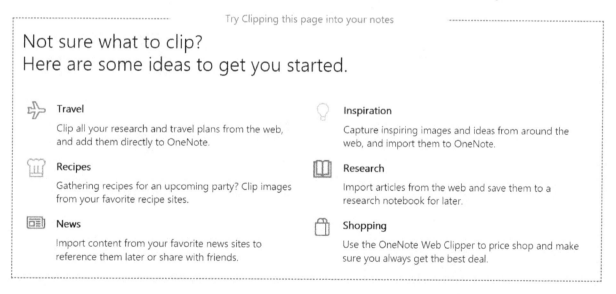

Figure 68

Step 4: To use, go to any website, for example, www.pricelesspctips.com (I love that site!), and click on the OneNote® icon at the top. You will be prompted to sign into your Microsoft or Work or School Account.

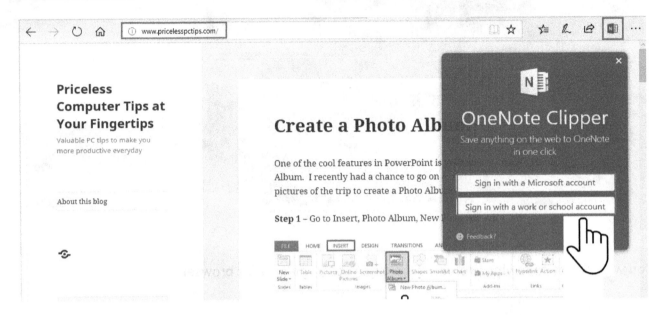

Figure 69

You will see the following options, to clip Full Page, Region, Article, or Bookmark. I chose Full Page and selected Clip. You can change the drop down under Location to change the location in your OneNote® where you want the clip to be inserted.

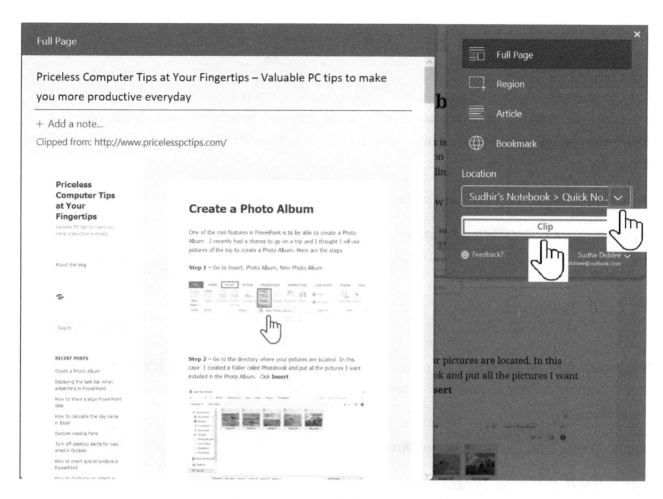

Figure 70

Figure 71

Click on **View in OneNote**® to see the clip inserted in the section you chose.

37. Print OneNote® to PDF

You can print any OneNote® page to PDF. This is useful when you want to send a document to someone who may not have OneNote®, or as an attachment to an email. When I archive the documents on my computer, I usually make a PDF of my OneNote® notebooks and file them away.

To do this, click on **File**, **Print**, and in the **Select Printer** option, select **Print to PDF.**

There you have your OneNote® notebook as a PDF printout.

38. Print Documents to OneNote®

Everyone is familiar with this pain point: printing receipts or confirmations for online purchases or reservations, which you must hold onto till the goods or services are delivered. OneNote® to the rescue!

Step 1: Create a photo album in OneNote®, on the Insert tab.

Step 2: Insert your saved images into the album.

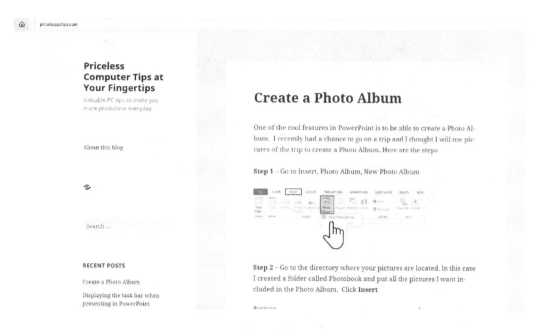

Figure 72

Step 3: Send them to print: in the **Select Printer** option, select **Send to OneNote.**

Figure 73

Step 4: Choose the section or page within OneNote where you will save your "printout."

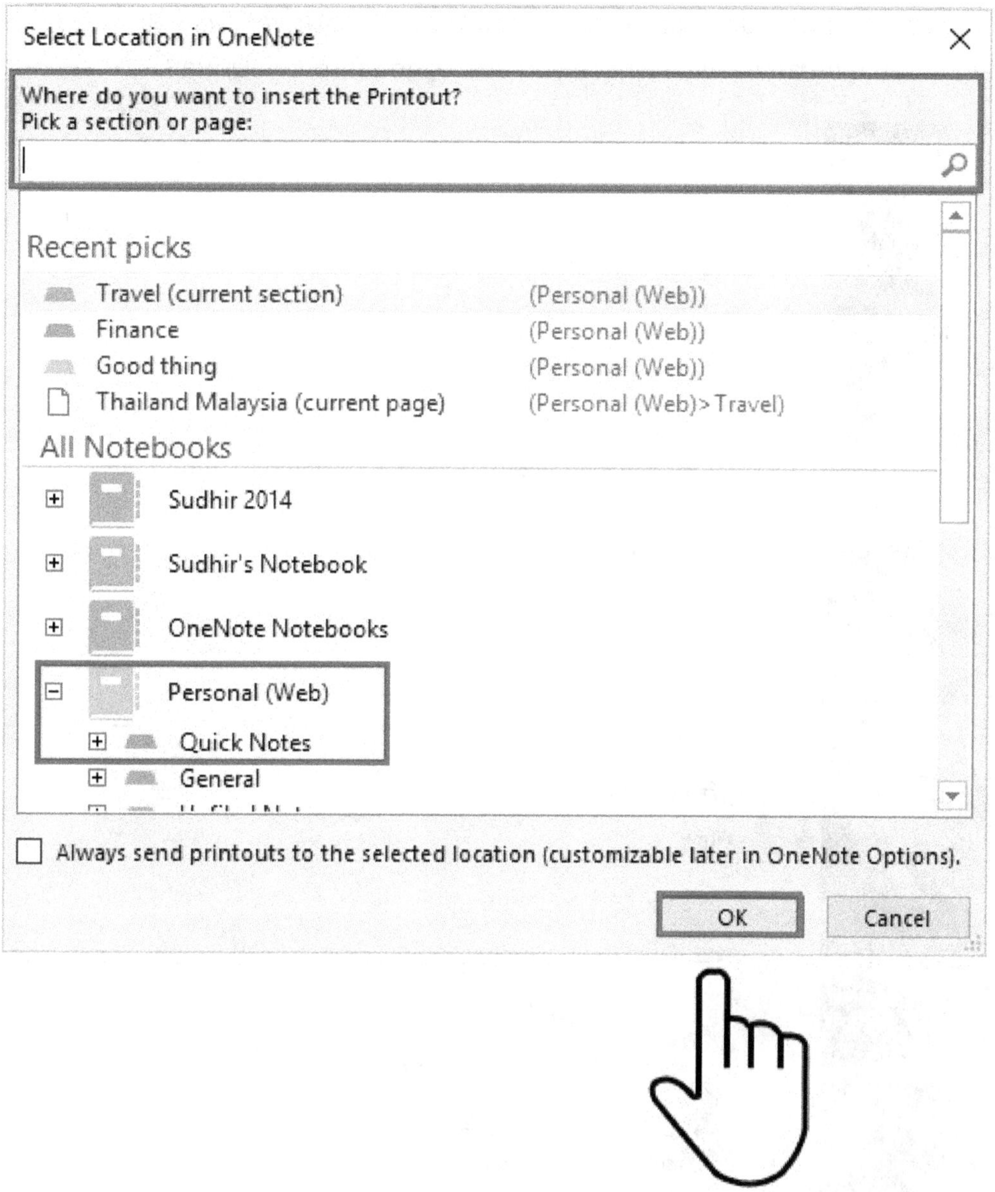

Figure 74

39. Storing notebooks on Microsoft OneDrive®

The VERY best part of OneNote® is that you can save the notebook in the cloud and access it from anywhere. To make Microsoft's cloud solution, OneDrive®, your backup for all your OneNote® notebooks, go to Account Information (user name and password needed) to add OneDrive® as a connected service, as below. Once you set your backup to OneDrive®, all your notes are secure and instantly available on any device where you are logged into OneDrive®.

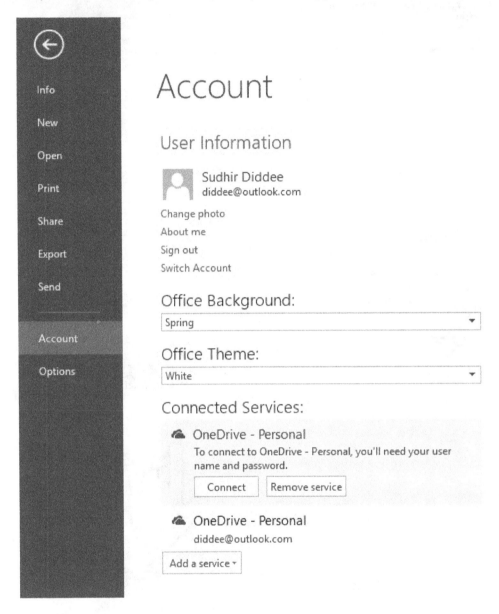

Figure 75

40. Sharing a notebook

You can share an entire notebook with another person. Here is how to do it:

Step 1 - Go to **File**, **Share**

Step 2 – Scroll over to **Share** and choose one of the options, such as **Invite People**

Step 3 – Enter the email address of the recipient and decide on the rights, e.g.: they can edit, or they can just view

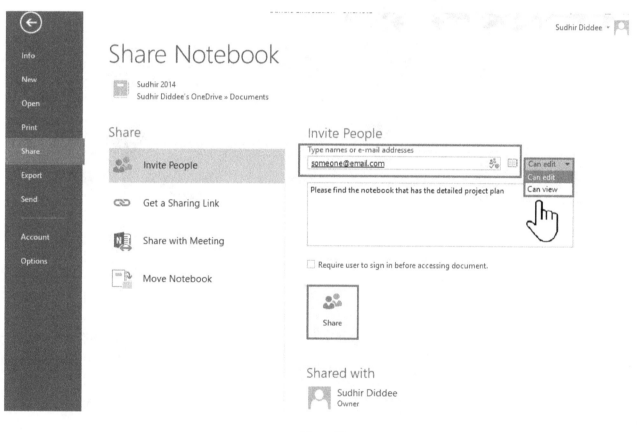

Figure 76

41. OneNote®.com

Here is a hidden secret that most of the regular OneNote® users are unaware of. It is called OneNote®.com. Think of it as a cloud repository of all your OneNote® notebooks.

You will need your Microsoft Account to sign in.

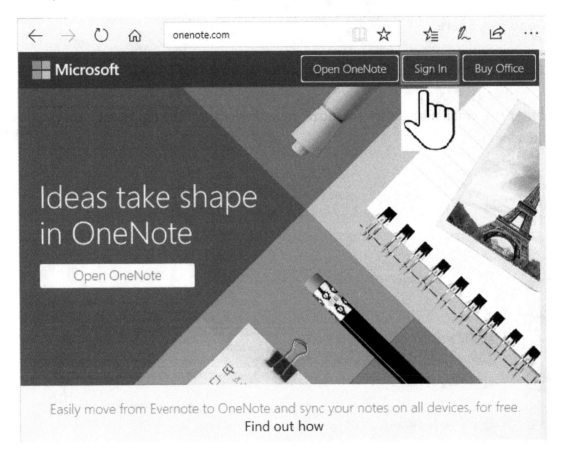

Figure 77

Here you will see a listing of all the OneNote® notebooks associated with your Microsoft Account. You can manage and delete Notebooks/Sections/Pages, and best of all, Search through all of your notebook contents.

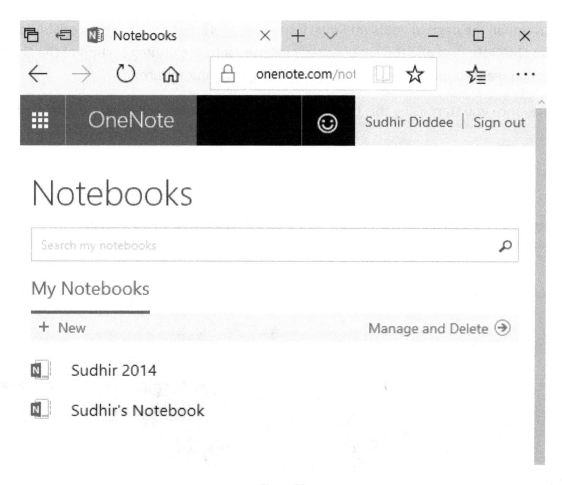

Figure 78

So, no matter what device you are on, if you ever need to find anything you have captured in OneNote®, just sign in and you can search your notebooks for the text or information.

42. Send notes to yourself

Here is another cool trick. Often you will have a situation where you get an email or information that you want to save. Say you just booked a trip and you have the confirmation in email. Since you want all the information in OneNote®, you would have to copy and paste the email contents into OneNote®, or launch OneNote® either on the desktop or log into the online version to save the information.

Easier: just email the page to yourself! Email it to me@OneNote.com from the registered email address on OneNote.com and the email will get inserted into the unfiled section of the OneNote® notebook that was last used. Then you can look through at your leisure.

Believe me, once you start using this trick, your usage of OneNote® will grow exponentially.

43. Send webpages to OneNote®

You can easily send webpages to OneNote. In the Windows® 10 browser Microsoft Edge®, there is a small icon to share the current website or page with someone.

Step 1: Click on the **sharing icon**, as shown below:

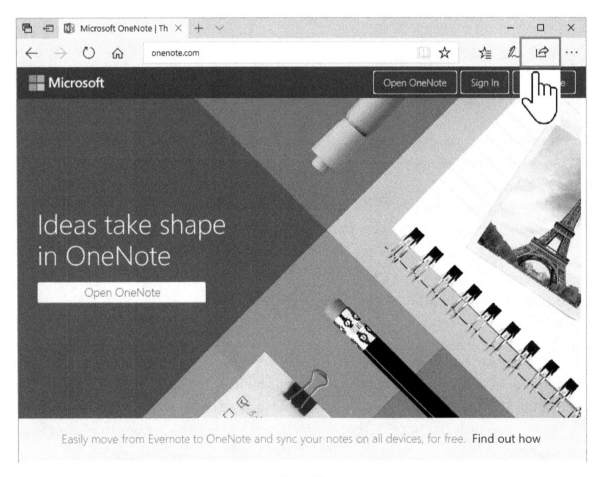

Figure 79

Step 2: Click on the **OneNote® icon** in the share options, to share the webpage with OneNote®.

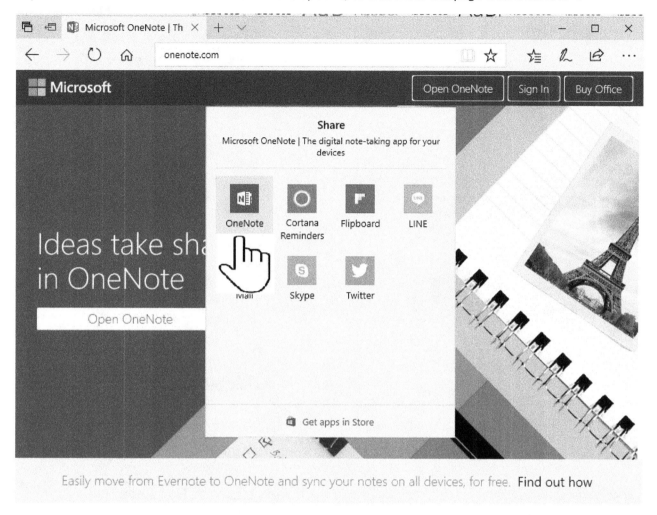

Figure 80

Step 3: Add a quick note so that you can find it. You can use the drop-down arrow to see where the note will be inserted. Hit **Send**. By default it lands in Unfiled notes section

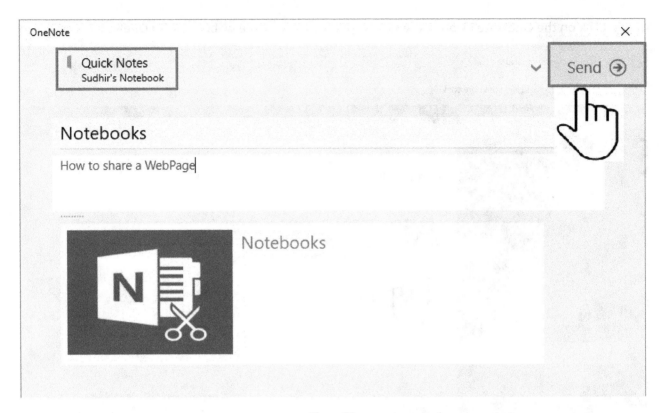

Figure 81

44. Translate in OneNote®

You can translate text from several languages via the built-in Microsoft Translator. Here is how to do the translation:

Step 1: Highlight the text you want to translate and right-click, then select **Translate** from the pop-up menu, as shown below.

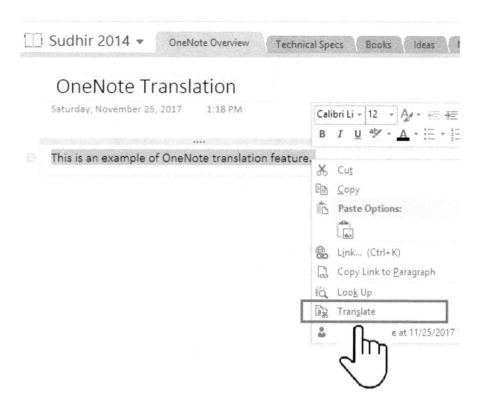

Figure 82

You can see the translation in the research window that opens as shown below. Note that in this case it translates the sentence from English to French:

Figure 83

45. Insert Excel into OneNote®

One of the improvements in OneNote® over the years is the ability to insert a new or existing spreadsheet, or the charts or graphs from within a spreadsheet. Simply choose **Insert, Spreadsheet,** and the type of spreadsheet you wish to insert.

Figure 84

When you click on the edit button, below, a new instance of Excel starts within OneNote® which allows you to edit the spreadsheet.

Insert Excel in OneNote

Insert Excel in OneNote - Spreadsheet

Figure 85

Note that you need to have a copy of Microsoft Excel or a subscription to Office® 365 for Excel to work on your machine.

46. Microsoft Edge® Browser Web Note

With Microsoft Edge you can take notes on a web page and the note automatically gets inserted in your default OneNote® notebook. This is incredibly powerful when you are collaborating with someone and want to annotate on a page and get feedback. It is best explained by the example below.

Say you have a website and it uses the term "Sign in," and you want your design team to change it to "Log in."

Step 1: Below, say you are on your website using Microsoft Edge® as your browser. Choose the icon, **Add Notes.**

Figure 86

Step 2: Choose the option, **Add a Note**.

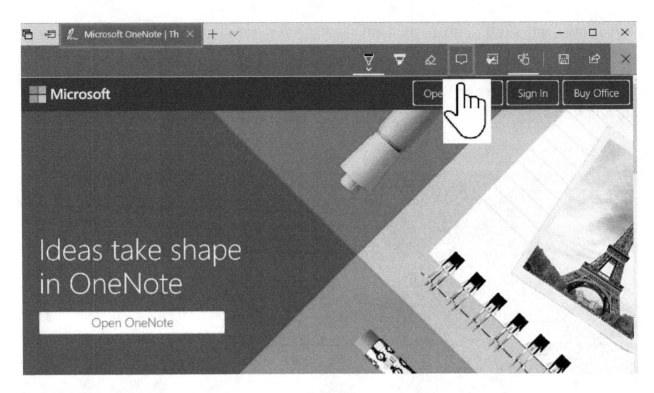

Figure 87

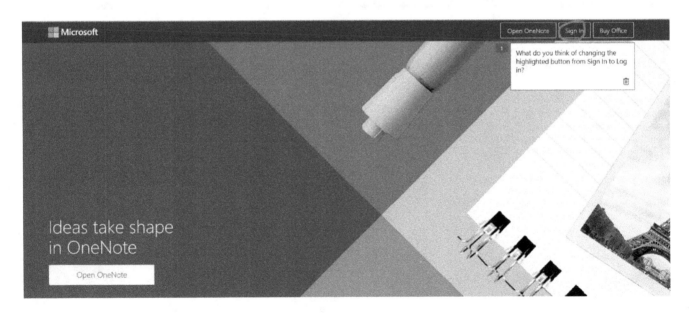

Figure 88

Step 3: Save your note to OneNote's® Quick Notes section:

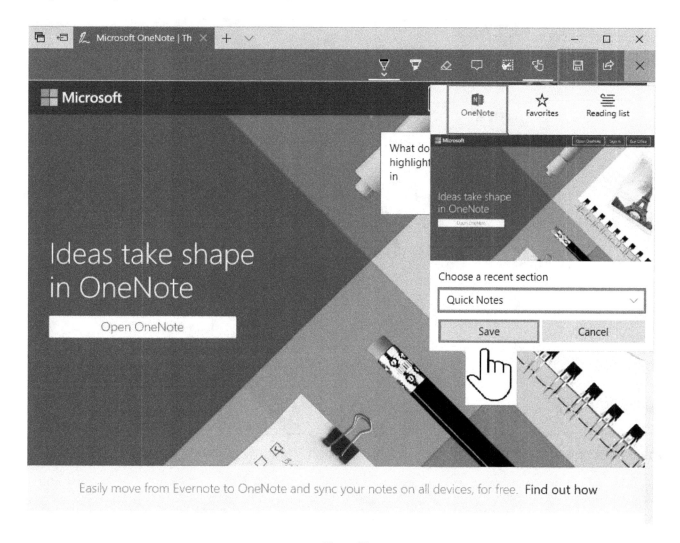

Figure 89

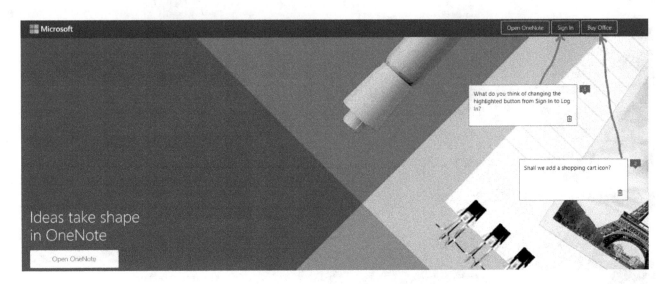

Figure 90

47. Linked note taking

You can link your notes to ensure consistency if you want the notes to appear in two notebooks. To do so, just click on **Review**, then **Linked Notes** from within your active page, and select where you want the linked notes to appear.

Linked Note

Saturday, November 25, 2017   4:14 PM

Here is an example of linked Notes in One Note

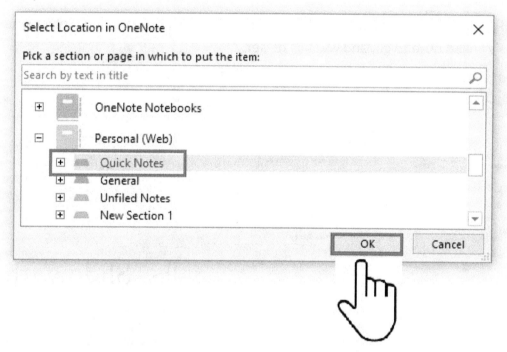

Figure 91

Click **OK** and your notes will be linked.

48. Take notes on PowerPoint® slides

You can even take notes for a PowerPoint® slide. Just launch an existing PowerPoint slide and click on **Review, Linked Notes**.

Figure 92

Step 2 – When you click on Linked Notes you will get a pop-up menu. Select where you want the slide's linked note to go, and you will be set.

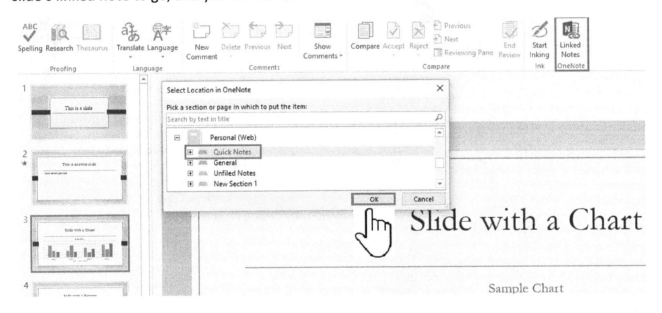

Figure 93

49. Send to blog

If you are an avid blogger, you can blog directly from OneNote®. Just link OneNote® to your blog. Here are the steps to follow:

Step 1 – Go to **File, Send, Send to Blog**

Figure 94

It will open a dialog to Register a Blog Account. Select **Register Now**.

Figure 95

Step 2 – Enter your account information and follow the steps to directly publish your blog from OneNote®.

Figure 96

50. Screen clipping

This is one of the cool features which makes Microsoft OneNote® one of my favorite products. When you are on a website or a program and you want to capture a snippet of the site and file it for reference, you can capture screenshots of what you see. This is especially useful for Web research, trip planning, online shopping, and product comparisons.

Here are the steps:

Step 1 - Insert a screen clipping from the web: press **Windows Logo Key + S while** in any program or browser.

Step 2 - Select an area of your screen. A separate OneNote® window will open to display the Unfiled Notes section where the screen clipping is inserted:

Figure 97

Here is how it is embedded:

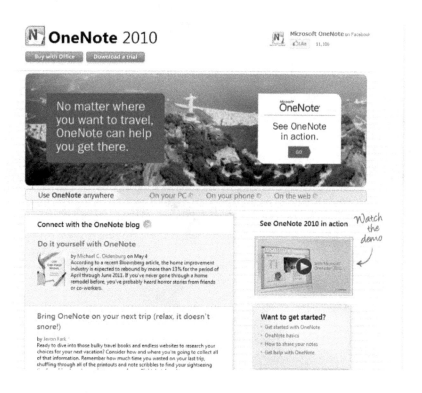

Figure 98

Microsoft OneNote® 2010 - Planner and note-taking software – www.Office.com
http://office.microsoft.com/en-us/OneNote/

Screen clipping taken: 7/10/2011 10:07 AM

Hint: If you want to insert a screen clipping into the current page instead of the Unfiled Notes section, switch to the Microsoft OneNote® window, put the cursor where you want the clipping, and click Insert > Screen Clipping, or the Clip button on the toolbar:

Figure 99

51. Quick bullets in Microsoft OneNote®

If you want to have bullet points in your notes, you can just type **CTRL + the period key "."** The text appears as a bulleted list. If you want the list to appear as numbers instead of bullets, type **CTRL + the slash key "/"**.

52. Attach files to Microsoft OneNote®

OneNote® has become the default collection application for me. One reason: often when you take notes, research on a topic, or want to save an attachment, you would prefer all the related files/applications on the same page.

An example would be the large amount of information you can accumulate for a trip, such as reservations for the hotel or airport parking, etc.

You can attach the actual files/PDFs right on the page.

Here is a sample trip page for a trip from Seattle to Sydney:

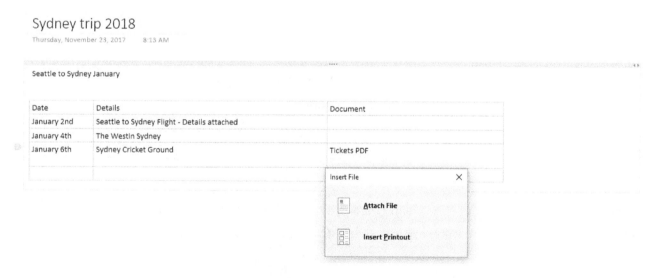

Figure 100

Here is how the page appears with the attachments:

Sydney trip 2018

Thursday, November 23, 2017   8:13 AM

Seattle to Sydney January

Date	Details	Document
January 2nd	Seattle to Sydney Flight - Details attached	Flight Confirmation # AXZ4JT
January 4th	The Westin Sydney	Sydney_Ho...
January 6th	Sydney Cricket Ground	Tickets PDF SCG Venue Map
January 4th -10th	Sydney Train Map	SydneyTrai...

Figure 101

Simply drag and drop any file from Windows Explorer® onto a page in Microsoft OneNote®, or insert it by using **Insert > Files** on the OneNote® menu.

You can open and edit an attached file by double-clicking its file icon.

You can also attach a printout directly in OneNote®, like the Sydney Train Map below. So this way, you can have the entire itinerary in a single document for your trip.

Sydney trip 2018

Thursday, November 23, 2017   8:13 AM

Seattle to Sydney January

Date	Details	Document
January 2nd	Seattle to Sydney Flight - Details attached	Flight Confirmation # AXZ4JT
January 4th	The Westin Sydney	Sydney_Ho...
January 6th	Sydney Cricket Ground	Tickets PDF SCG Venue Map
January 4th -10th	Sydney Train Map	SydneyTrai...

Metro Map Printout

SydneyTrain_Map

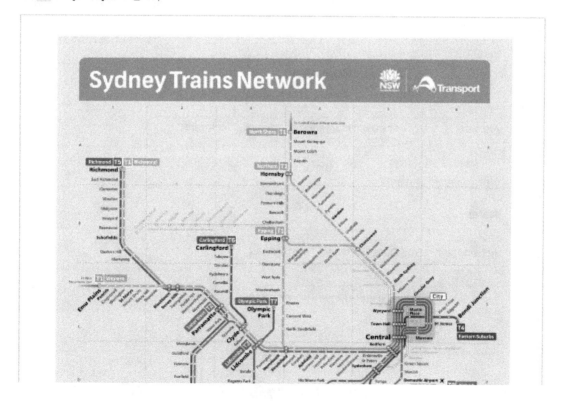

Figure 102

This feature of OneNote® is invaluable when you research a project and want to collect all related info in one place that is easily accessible.

Think of it like this – if you are working on a new product plan, you can have the entire plan and all associated links in one place – spreadsheets for financials, PDFs for the advertising campaign, PowerPoint documents and Word® documents, calendar meetings, contact info, **everything** related to the plan in one place, in Microsoft OneNote®.

53. Insert OneNote® tables "on the fly"

Sometimes when you are taking notes, you need to insert a table to capture information in a grid. Type in your text and hit the **Tab** key. A table will magically appear—and if you hit tab, you can add additional columns.

When you want to create a row, just hit enter:

Write a book on Aliens

Saturday, October 30, 2010
10:00 AM

Subject	Write a book on Aliens
Date and Location	Saturday, October 30, 2010 10:00 AM - 12:00 PM
Attendees	Sudhir Diddee, Shreya R, Kory, Jill M., S Mehrotra, R.Shankar
Message	

Link to Outlook item

Notes

Action Item	Due Date	Owner	Notes

Figure 103

54. OneNote® Class Notebook Add-in

This new free add-in for the Microsoft OneNote® desktop (2013 or 2016) is designed to increase teacher efficiency. It includes page and section distribution, quick review of student work, and assignment and grading integration with third-party services.

It is an add-in for OneNote® desktop (2013 or 2016) and is built into Windows® for Mac and Windows® 10.

Download the add-in: https://www.OneNote.com/classnotebook.

Once you download you will see a new tab, **Class Notebook:**

Figure 104

Click on **Connections** and you will be prompted to connect to several third-party services so that you can aggregate all information in one place.

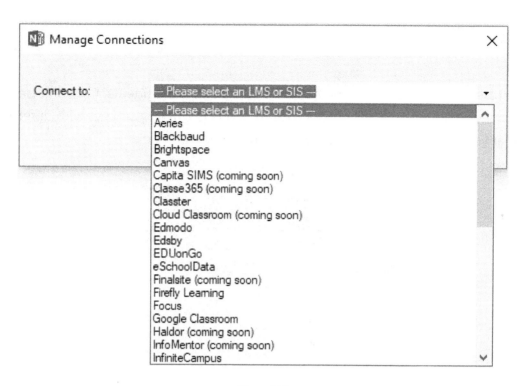

Figure 105

55. Stickers in OneNote®

One new feature in OneNote®: stickers that teachers can give to students. Click on Insert and you will see a "smiley." Clicking on it will open a stickers window, offering smileys with different messages that you can insert into your students' OneNote® notebooks.

Figure 106

Extra

1. Evernote® to OneNote® Importer

If you have notes in Evernote®, you can migrate them over to OneNote® seamlessly. Just download the tool and follow the directions. Here is the link to start your migration:

https://www.onenote.com/import-evernote-to-onenoteError! Hyperlink reference not valid.

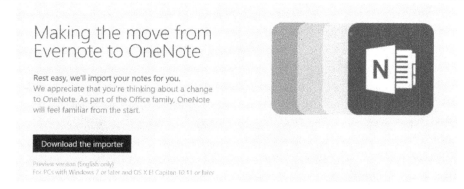

Figure 107

2. Office® Lens

Think of Office Lens as a scanner in your pocket. For FREE!!. While this may be an odd addition to a book on OneNote®, you are going to thank me for it. Go to www.OfficeLens.com and download the app.

Prerequisites - a smartphone capable of taking clear pictures; the OneNote® app downloaded on your smart phone.

Figure 108

References and Useful sites

1. Chris Pratley's Blog - OneNote® genesis
   https://blogs.msdn.microsoft.com/chris_pratley/2004/01/30/onenote-genesis/

2. Microsoft Education Blog
   https://techcommunity.microsoft.com/t5/Education-Blog/The-best-version-of-OneNote-on-Windows/ba-p/183726

3. Microsoft Office® 365 OneNote® blog
   https://www.microsoft.com/en-us/microsoft-365/blog/onenote/page/2/

Microsoft OneNote® Shortcuts

Task	Shortcut
Open a new OneNote® window.	CTRL+M
Open a small OneNote® window to create a side note.	CTRL+SHIFT+M or Windows+ALT+N
Dock the OneNote® window.	CTRL+ALT+D
Insert a link.	CTRL+K
Apply or remove bulleted list formatting from the selected paragraph.	CTRL+PERIOD
Apply or remove numbered list formatting from the selected paragraph.	CTRL+SLASH
Apply a Heading 1 style to the current note.	CTRL+ALT+1
Apply a Heading 2 style to the current note.	CTRL+ALT+2
Insert the current date.	ALT+SHIFT+D
Insert the current date and time.	ALT+SHIFT+F
Apply, mark, or clear the To Do tag.	CTRL+1
Apply or clear the Important tag.	CTRL+2
Apply or clear the Question tag.	CTRL+3
Apply or clear the Remember for later tag.	CTRL+4
Enable or disable full page view.	F11
Open a new OneNote® window.	CTRL+M
Expand or collapse the tabs of a page group.	CTRL+SHIFT+*
Enable or disable full page view.	F11
Move the insertion point to the **Search** box to search all notebooks.	CTRL+E
Send the selected pages in an email message.	CTRL+SHIFT+E
Create a **Today** Outlook® task from the currently selected note.	CTRL+SHIFT+1
Create a **Tomorrow** Outlook® task from the currently selected note.	CTRL+SHIFT+2
Create a **This Week** Outlook® task from the currently selected note.	CTRL+SHIFT+3
Lock all password-protected sections.	CTRL+ALT+L

Full list of shortcuts in available on Office.com